EX[...]
Sa[...] [...]
Jenny Doan, David Mifsud

MANAGING EDITOR
Natalie Earnheart

CREATIVE DIRECTOR
Christine Ricks

PHOTOGRAPHER
BPD Studios

CONTRIBUTING PHOTOGRAPHERS
Jake Doan

VIDEOGRAPHER
Jake Doan

DESIGNER & TECHNICAL WRITER
Linda Johnson

PROJECT DESIGN TEAM
Natalie Earnheart, Jenny Doan,
Sarah Galbraith

AUTHOR OF PATCHWORK MURDER
Steve Westover

CONTRIBUTING COPY WRITERS
Katie Mifsud, Jenny Doan, Camille Maddox,
Natalie Earnheart, Christine Ricks, Alan
Doan, Sarah Galbraith

COPY EDITOR
Geoff Openshaw

CONTRIBUTING PIECERS
Jenny Doan, Natalie Earnheart,
Kelly McKenzie, Cindy Morris

CONTRIBUTING QUILTERS
Bernice Kelly, Deloris Burnett, Jamey Stone,
Betty Bates, Sherry Melton, Amber Weeks,
Sandi Gaunce, Daniela Kirk, Amy Gertz, Mari
Zullig, Megan Gilliam, Mary Bontrager, Karen
Russell

Cenveo Publisher Services
2901 Byrdhill Road
Richmond, VA 23228

CONTACT US
Missouri Star Quilt Co
114 N Davis
Hamilton, Mo. 64644
888-571-1122
info@missouriquiltco.com

BLOCK Idea Book™ Winter Volume 2 Issue 1
©2015 All Rights Reserved by Missouri Star Quilt
Company. Reproduction in whole or in part in
any language without written permission from
Missouri Star Quilt Company or BLOCK Idea Book
is prohibited. No one may copy, reprint or distribute
any of the patterns or materials in this magazine for
commercial use without written permission of
Missouri Star Quilt Company. Anything you make
using our patterns or ideas is your business, do
whatever you want with the stuff you make, it's yours!

content

HELLO
from MSQC

Welcome to the second year of BLOCK! We hope you enjoyed the issues of 2014. We had a wonderful time putting them together!

When we first decided to create our very own magazine, it was a huge and daunting undertaking. We'd done a lot over the years, but we'd yet to venture into print magazines. It was scary! We worked harder, stayed up later, and had more fun than ever before. It's been quite the adventure! You just never know what you are capable of unless you try!

Likewise, this year we encourage you to try something you have never done before. Be brave. Work to conquer a roadblock. You can do it! Don't tell yourself you can't. You can!

Of course, you can't take on every challenge at once. Life gets so hectic and, if you're not careful, it's easy to feel overwhelmed and discouraged. Focus on mastering just one thing at a time and don't forget to take care of yourself in the process. We are givers but we can't give if our bucket is empty! So do something every day that fills your bucket and keep smiling! Welcome to 2015!

Jenny

JENNY DOAN
MISSOURI STAR QUILT CO

fabric is in the air

This month always gets my skin itching for spring. The long, dark winter days are almost over and the birds begin to return and chirp their sweet songs. I eagerly await the sounds of melting snow and the fresh, earthy smells of the damp ground around me. It's like my senses come to life again and I can hear, smell and almost taste that spring is just around the corner.

I think we can all agree that new fabric can have the same endorphin releasing power as a sunny spring day. And maybe chocolate too. All these things make me happy, and when I feel happy I have a renewed desire to create something new. I've taken some of my favorite spring solids and paired them with some really fresh prints. I hope this will release your creative bug and get you inspired to make something new.

CHRISTINE RICKS
MSQC Creative Director, BLOCK MAGAZINE

SOLIDS

FBY12461 Kona Cotton - Mint
by Robert Kaufman Fabrics for Robert Kaufman
SKU: K001-1234

FBY13026 Cotton Supreme Solids - Neon
by RJR Fabrics for RJR Fabrics
SKU: 9617-348

FBY8523 Cotton Supreme Solids - Carnation
by RJR Fabrics for RJR Fabrics
SKU: 9617-135

FBY8533 Cotton Supreme Solids - Rhododendron
by RJR Fabrics for RJR Fabrics
SKU: 9617-181

FBY12413 Kona Cotton - Everglade
by Robert Kaufman Fabrics for Robert Kaufman
SKU: K001-356

FBY3695 Kona Cotton - Berry Yardage
by Robert Kaufman Fabrics for Robert Kaufman
SKU: K001-1016

PRINTS

FBY18656 Cotton + Steel Basics - XO Toy Boat
by Cotton + Steel for RJR Fabrics
SKU: 5001-009

FBY19544 Moxi-Saavy Stripes Marshmallow Acid Green
by Studio M for Moda Fabrics
SKU: 32965 19

FBY20052 Paper Dolls Bakery - Gingham Pink
by Sibling Arts Studio for Riley Blake
SKU: C4356-PINK

FBY18226 Best. Day. Ever! - Raspberry Playing Field
by April Rosenthal for Moda Fabrics
SKU: 24011 13

FBY15252 Avant Garden - Aqua Skies
by MoMo for Moda Fabrics
SKU: 16121 13

FBY14084 Gem Tones - Ta Dot Jewel
by Michael Miller Fabrics for Michael Miller
SKU: CX1492-JEWE-D

For the tutorial and everything you need to make this quilt visit: www.msqc.co/blockwinter15

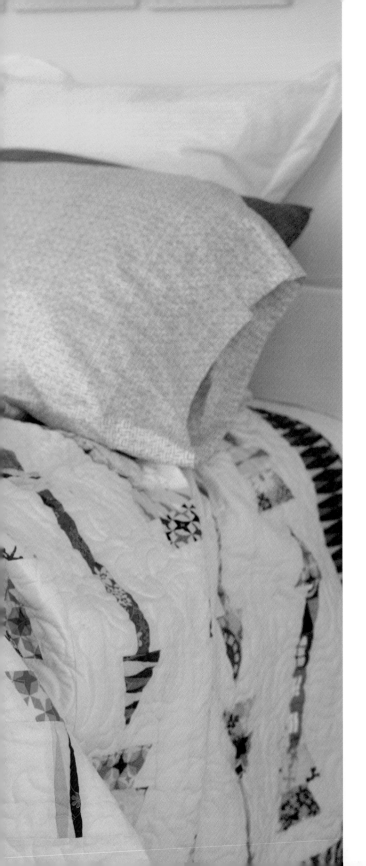

hit the mark

quilt designed by NATALIE EARNHEART

One year, my high school offered an alternative to traditional phys ed - archery - and I thought, "Alright! Sign me up! How hard can it be? Bow, arrow, target, done." Imagine my surprise when the first day of class found me with a bow in one hand and the string for it in the other. We started from square one learning how to string our own bows. Then we moved on to detailed instruction about arrows, the effect of feathers, the basic physics of a straight shot, and what felt like an unabridged history of archery from the dawn of time.

Then came my moment to finally shoot the bow. Remember how I thought archery would be "Bow, arrow, target"? That first time it was more like "Bow, arrow, flop." You might think I'd be discouraged, but I was hooked. I actually enjoyed practicing and got better and better. There was even one time I loosed the bow and the string took the skin on my arm with it, but I liked to think it just made me tougher.

Studying archery was very satisfying and fun, but I didn't realize how valuable it was to me until my own little boys begged me to learn. So one day, we went out into the forest together and searched for the best sticks to make their own bows and arrows. I remember very clearly teaching them that if they wanted their arrows to fly true, they needed straight sticks. As I watched them search for the perfect sticks for arrows, I couldn't help but think about how lucky I was to be their mother, and to be there to watch them grow and develop.

I love the quote that says, "An arrow can only be shot by pulling it backward. So, when life is dragging you back with its difficulties, its going to launch you into something great." My experiences with archery and motherhood have taught me many things. This quilt reminds me to keep focused, aim straight for your goal, and don't let fear get in the way.

" An arrow can only be shot by pulling it backward. So, when life is dragging you back with its difficulties, its going to launch you into something great. "

materials

makes a 86" X 87" quilt

QUILT TOP
- (1) 10" square pack print
- 2 yds background solid
- 1½ yds outer border

BINDING
- ¾ yd coordinating fabric

BACKING
- 8 yds 44" **OR** 2¾ yds 108"

ADDITIONAL TOOLS
- MSQC 5" Half-Hexagon Shape
- MSQC Small Simple Wedge

SAMPLE QUILT
- **Playful** by Melody Miller of Cotton + Steel for RJR
- **Bella Solids Natural (12)** by Moda Fabrics

1 cut

From (40) 10" print squares cut:
    (1) 1½" strip *(shaft)*
    (2) 5" half hexagons *(feathers)*
    (1) 5" small wedge *(arrow)* **1A**

From background solid fabric cut:
    (6) 10" WOF strips; subcut into
        (80) 3" segments *(shaft)*
    (6) 7½" WOF strips; subcut into
        (40) 6" segments *(arrow)*
    (5) 5" WOF strips; subcut into
        (80) 2½" segments; cut a
        half hexie from each; then in
        half again *(feathers)* **1B**
    (24) 2½" WOF strips *(sashing/ inner border—SSIB)*

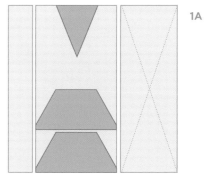

1A

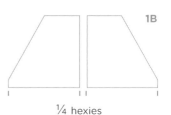

1B

¼ hexies

2 arrowheads

Build an arrowhead with (1) print wedge and (1) 7½" x 6" background block. Center the bottom of the wedge on a 7½" side. **2A** Fold the background fabric over one side of the wedge. Press and sew ¼" seam along the fold. **2B** Press open. Repeat for the second side of the wedge. **2C** Square up arrowhead block to 6" x 5." **2D**

2A

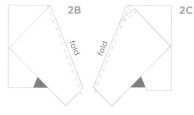

2B   2C

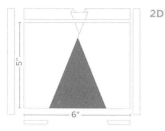

2D

3 shaft

Sew (2) 3" x 10" background rectangles lengthwise to either side of the 1½" x 10" print rectangle. Trim to 6" x 10." **3A**

4 feathers

Sew (2) quarter hexies to either side of a half-hexie. **4A** Make 2. Stack them one on top of the other and sew together. Trim to 6" x 4½." **4B**

5 build an arrow

Use (1) arrowhead block, (1) shaft & (1) feather block to build an arrow. Attach an arrowhead and feather block to either end of the shaft, sewing across the 6" side. Press. Make 40. **5A**

Block size: 6" x 18½"

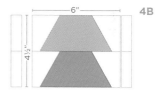

3A

4A

4B

5B

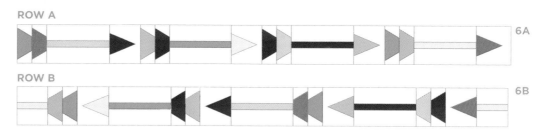

ROW A

6A

ROW B

6B

6 row construction

The quilt consists of 2 alternating rows, **A** & **B**, with 4 arrows in each row facing the same direction and 2½" sashing between the rows.

Row A: Sew 4 arrows together end-to-end. Make (5). Press. **6A**

Row B: Sew 3 arrows end-to-end; cut the fourth in half and add the feather section in front of an arrowhead; the arrowhead half behind a feather. Make (5). **6B**

Piece (20) SSIB strips together end-to-end. Subcut into (11) 73" lengths. Attach a strip to the bottom of each row. Trim

13

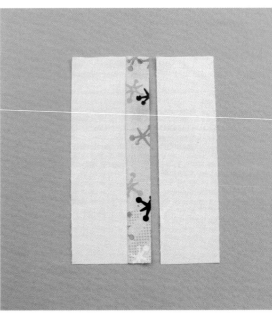

1   Build an arrowhead by folding the background fabric over one side of the wedge. Sew a ¼" seam along the fold. Step 2.

2   Press open and repeat for the opposite side. Step 2.

3   To make an arrow's shaft, sew (2) 3" x 10" background rectangles to either side of a print 1½" x 10" rectangle. Step 3.

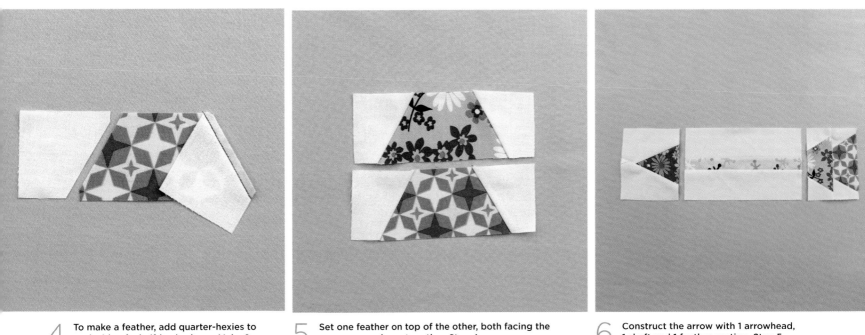

4   To make a feather, add quarter-hexies to each side of a half-hexie shape. Make 2. Step 4.

5   Set one feather on top of the other, both facing the same way and sew together. Step 4.

6   Construct the arrow with 1 arrowhead, 1 shaft and 1 feather section. Step 5.

excess. Going forward, press all seams to the sashing or borders.

7 arrange & sew

Lay out the quilt beginning with a **B** row, arrows facing left. Next add an **A** row, arrows facing right and so on.

Sew each row to the one below, lining up the left hand edge. The **A** rows will be slightly longer on the right hand side. Add the last 73" SSIB strip to the top.

8 complete borders

Straighten the right edge. **8A** Measure the quilt top length. Piece and subcut the remaining (4) SSIB strips to that size—one for each side. Attach both to the quilt.

Quilt Center w/IB: 76½" x 77½"

From the outer border fabric cut (9) 5" strips. Follow steps in *construction basics* to attach to the quilt. Press to the borders.

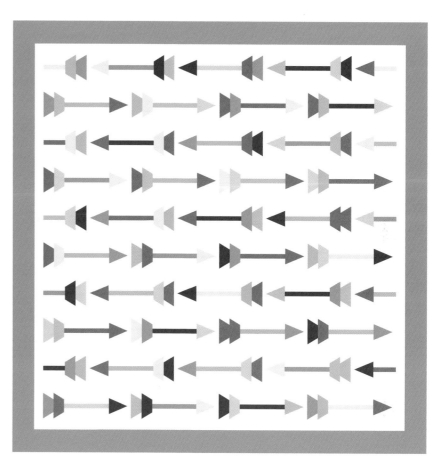

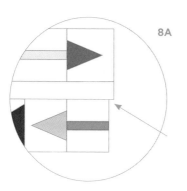

8A

9 quilt & bind

Layer quilt top on batting and backing and quilt the way you like. Square up all raw edges.

Cut (9) 2½" strips from binding fabric to finish. See *construction basics* for greater detail.

For the tutorial and everything you need to make this quilt visit:
www.msqc.co/blockwinter15

disappearing hourglass 2

quilt designed by JENNY DOAN

The simplicity of youth often leads us to make improbable goals. For example, I had my entire life mapped out by the tender age of thirteen. Armed with a wealth of knowledge gathered from Disney and Mayberry, I created an image of the perfect fairytale life, complete with a perpetually tiny waist and the most gallant of knights in shining armor as my suitor.

I was determined to live in a charming little yellow house with a white picket fence that wrapped all the way around a flawlessly manicured lawn. I even picked out the perfect married name to complete the fantasy: Jenny Livingston.

Now here was the problem: I didn't actually know a single soul by the name of Livingston. There was no dreamy Livingston boy down the street; I just thought that Jenny Livingston had a nice, classy ring to it. I remember spending many long hours in my biology class doodling "Jenny Livingston" again and again in my notebook. I developed quite the elegant signature for my imaginary adult self!

Well, a few years have gone by, and, not surprisingly, those exact dreams never did come to pass. No yellow house, no "Jenny Livingston," not even the tiny waist! But as I look back over the years, I am filled with gratitude for the life I do have. How could any yellow house even begin to compare with the wonderful experiences I have shared with my husband and our seven children? Thank goodness life rarely goes according to plan! Dreaming about the future sure is fun, but I think the secret to finding your real "Happily Ever After" is as simple as traveling along the road of life and learning to love whatever comes your way.

I feel the same way about these disappearing blocks. I make a block, cut it up, and put it together again. I never know what I'm going to get. There is no pattern. I don't have one of those fancy computer programs to help me visualize different variations. I just have to go ahead and give it a try and see what happens! It's such fun, I doubt I'll ever tire of creating new and different disappearing blocks! After all, what's the fun in only getting exactly what you expect? Jenny Livingston would never have understood this.

materials

makes a 59" X 70¼" quilt

QUILT TOP
- 1½ yds dark solid
- 1½ yds background solid
- ½ yd inner border
- 1 yd outer border

BINDING
- ½ yd coordinating fabric

BACKING
- 4 yds coordinating fabric

SAMPLE QUILT
- **Bella Solids White (98) & Sky (177)** by Moda Fabrics

1 cut & sew

From the background and dark solid yardage cut: (5) 10" WOF strips; subcut into (20) 10" squares for each color.

Pair (2) 10" squares RST (right sides together)—one background solid, one dark solid. **1A** Sew a ¼" seam all around.

2 cut

Sometimes this step goes faster with a rotating cutting mat. With your rotary cutter cut across the pair diagonally twice. Yield: 4 half square triangles (HST). Press seams to the dark solid fabric. Repeat with 20 pairs total.

1A

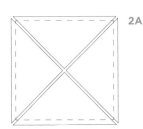

2A

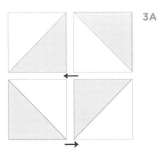

3A

with a center seam. Cut 2⅛" away from the center seam on both sides, turning the block as needed without disturbing it. **4A** This is where a rotating cutting mat comes in handy. Repeat for the other center seam.

2⅛" 4¼"

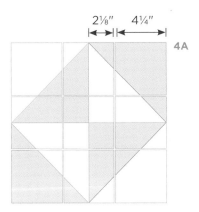

4A

5 turn & sew

Turn each of the 4 corner squares 180;° the center 90.° Study the diagram. **5A** Sew the 3 blocks of each row together first. Follow pressing arrows. Then sew rows together. If all seams have been pressed to the dark solid fabric the seams should nest easily.

Block size: 11¾" x 11¾"
Yield: 20 blocks

3 hourglass block

Arrange the 4 HSTs to create an hourglass in the center. Follow the diagram. **3A** Sew HSTs in rows first RST. Press to the dark solid side. Sew the two rows together nesting the center seam. *(Follow pressing arrows)* Make 20.

4 cut

Square up the hourglass to 12¾" symetrically. This will make cutting in thirds much easier. Each of the 9 squares will measure 4¼." This measurement divided by 2 (=2⅛") will allow you to use the center seams as the cutting guides. Line up the ruler

6 layout & sew

Lay the blocks in a 4 x 5 setting. At this point, consider repressing seams for better nesting. **6A** Sew blocks together in rows; press these seams to the same side in even rows; to the opposite side in odd rows. Next, sew rows together to form the quilt center.

Quilt center: 45½" x 56¾"

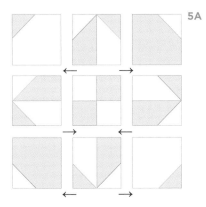

5A

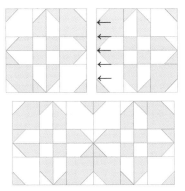

6A match same color fabrics from block to block throughout; a small floating square on point will appear; arrows show examples of seams that may need repressing to nest.

1   Make (4) half square triangles (HSTs) from a background solid and a dark solid pair of 10″ squares. Sew a ¼″ seam around the edge and cut diagonally across twice. Steps 1 & 2.

2   Arrange the 4 HSTs to form an hourglass on point. Sew rows together first; then attach the top to the bottom—just like a 4-patch. Step 3.

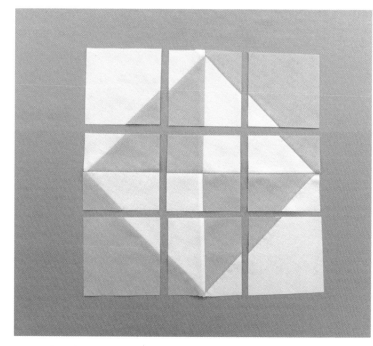

3   Squaring up the block to 12¾″ will make it easier to cut it into thirds. Measure 2⅛″ to cut each side of the center seam. The (9) individual blocks should measure 4¼″ square. Be careful not to move the block as you make your cuts. Step 4.

4   Turn each of the corner squares 180°; the center square 90°. Step 5.

A

C

D

B

7 borders

From the inner border fabric cut (6) 2½″ strips. Follow steps in *construction basics* to attach to the quilt. A-D Press to the borders.

Cut (6) 5″ strips of outer border fabric. Attach to the quilt in the same manner as the inner border.

8 quilt & bind

Layer quilt top on batting and backing and quilt the way you like. Square up all raw edges.

Cut (7) 2½″ strips from binding fabric to finish. See *construction basics* for more detail.

honey do

designed by NATALIE EARNHEART

We've never lived in a nice, new house. With a big family and a small income, the only way to find a home we could afford that was large enough to house the whole gang was to look for a real fixer-upper.

In some areas, renovating a home might entail little more than applying a fresh coat of paint and laying new carpet. In rural Missouri, however, you're lucky if you get to keep the original plumbing or floorboards!

It was a lot of work to transform an outdated, old house into a comfortable and attractive home, but there wasn't anything I wasn't willing try. (And with some clever encouragement, I could usually get my husband to pitch in as well!)

Back in those days, we didn't have entire television channels devoted to home improvement or YouTube tutorials to teach us how to do things, so I often headed out to a construction site to ask the workers for tips. Then I'd go home and give it a go.

For the tutorial and everything you need to make this quilt visit: **www.msqc.co/blockwinter15**

Perhaps I was feeling overzealous, but one day I decided I wanted to get rid of the nasty, old toilet in the bathroom. I took it out and set in the middle of the living room. When my husband walked in the room he stared at that toilet and then sighed, "Well, I guess we are replacing the toilet." He got right to work, and now we have a lovely new toilet in our bathroom!

One of the blessings of having to work so hard to have a pleasant home is that my children have grown up to be such resourceful adults. If they don't know how to do something,

they're not afraid to give it a shot anyway. They have accomplished so many incredible things just because they aren't afraid to try.

This willingness to try, despite the odds or preparedness, translates so well into quilting. While there may not be many new blocks out there, you can always find new ways to put them together. Don't be afraid to try something new. I'm sure you can create a quilt that is fresh, beautiful and totally unique. Trust your instincts and let your imagination run wild. You never know what you will come up with!

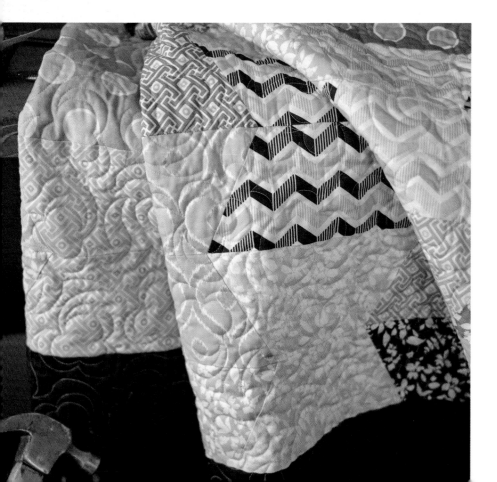

"While there may not be many new blocks out there, you can always find fun new ways to put them together."

materials

makes a 50½" X 63½" quilt

QUILT TOP
- (1) 10" print pack
- 1 yd dark solid fabric

BINDING
- ¾ yd coordinating fabric

BACKING
- 3¼ yds coordinating fabric

ADDITIONAL TOOLS
- 10" MSQC Half Hexagon Shape Tool

SAMPLE QUILT
- **Mixologie** by Studio M for Moda Fabrics
- **Bella Solids Navy (20)** by Moda Fabrics

1 cut & select

From the solid yardage cut:
- (3) 5" WOF strips; set aside.
- (3) 4⅝" WOF strips

With the *MSQC Half Hexagon Shape Tool* cut (13) half-hexies from the 4⅝" strips. Cut these in half to make quarter-hexies. **1A**

Cut (39) 10" squares in half once. Cut out shapes from the print rectangles. **1B** Keep same print shapes together.

2 arrange

Begin by laying out the print half-hexies in columns. Use 2 of the same print to make an hourglass shape by facing short sides toward each other. **2A** Stack 6

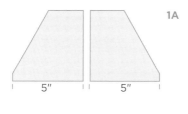

28

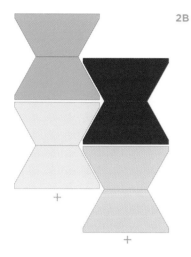

2B

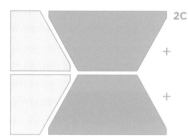

2C

hourglass shapes (=12 half-hexies) on top of each other for the first column.

Next, stagger the second column of 6 hourglass shapes so that they nestle into the first hourglasses. 2B

Repeat these 2 columns 3 times for a total of 6 columns of staggered hour-glasses.

Fill in the empty spaces at the top and bottom with the remaining half-hexies.

Center Setting: 6 x 13

Add a column of solid ¼-hexies before the first & after the last columns of hour-glasses. The final side edges will be straight. 2C

3 sew

Piece rows together first. Sew blocks RST offsetting the shapes at the ¼" seam allowance to make "dog ears." 3A & 3B Sew together. Press all seams in a row to the same side; seams in the next row to the opposite side and so on.

To complete the quilt center, sew rows together nesting seams as you go. Press horizontal seams away from the quilt's middle.

Quilt Center Size: 50" x 54"

3A

3B

4 borders

Measure the quilt top width in 3 places. Sew the 5" strips (that were set aside) together end-to-end. Cut (2) strips to the average of the 3 measurements. Attach to the top and bottom. Press to the borders.

5 quilt & bind

Layer quilt top on batting and backing and quilt the way you like. Square up all raw edges.

Cut (7) 2½" strips from binding fabric to finish. See *construction basics* for greater detail.

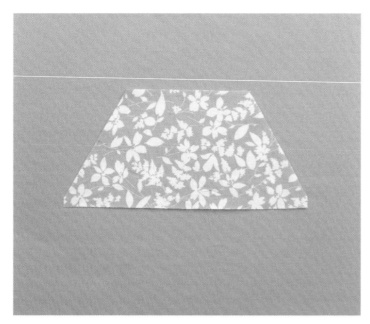

1 Cut (2) half-hexie shapes from each 10" square. You can cut the square in half first and layer the rectangles, or you can fold the square in half and remove the fold as you cut the shapes. Step 1.

2 Each half-hexie on the side of the quilt will have a solid quarter-hexie attached to it. Note how the sides are matched right sides together (RST). Check your positioning before sewing. Don't forget to make dog ears so the hexies line up correctly. Step 2.

3 The half-hexies are laid out so that short top and long bottom edges alternate creating straight rows. Step 2.

4 In subsequent rows match same-print half-hexies to form an hourglass. Hourglass pairs are staggered in order to nestle into each other. Step 2.

Love is in the air

designed by JENNY DOAN

You know how newlyweds can seem a bit corny with all that love stuff? My attitude has always been one of questioning why we should let the newlyweds have all the fun. Ron and I can be a little ridiculous at times, but hey, where's the fun in being sensible, especially when it comes to love?

We are both hopelessly romantic and, for us, Valentine's Day is a big deal. One of my favorite things is that while Ron buys me candy for Valentine's Day, he also gets some for all the kids, even now that they're grown. (I like to say that the extra sweets mean he's extra sweet.)

Back when we were first married, Ron rode a motorcycle to work. Valentine's Day was approaching and I thought my plan was so cute: I got him a giant three-foot mylar balloon that said "I Love You." I

For the tutorial and everything you need to make this quilt visit:
www.msqc.co/blockwinter15

sneaked over to his work to tie it to the handlebars while his motorcycle was parked outside. I didn't think twice about how he would get it home, but he liked it so much that he drove home ten miles an hour on backroads just so it wouldn't get ruined!

A few years after the balloon bliss we had a special dinner at our church for Valentine's Day. I had been thinking of ways to top the balloon bike, and boy did I ever! I surprised him in front of our friends by singing to him. And if you haven't already figured out how sappy we are this should tell you: I sang "Wind Beneath My Wings"!

You can see that Valentine's Day is a favorite of ours and I have a lot of fun with the corny, sweet things we do. However, even with all of these amusing tales of Valentine's Day cheesiness, nothing we do will ever top the first Valentine's Day we spent together, because that's the day Ron made me the happiest woman in the world by asking me to marry him. Now can you see why I love Valentine's Day so much?

" . . . but hey, where's the fun in being sensible, especially when it comes to love? "

materials

makes a 31" X 31" wallhanging

QUILT TOP
- (1) 10" pack of valentine-themed fabrics
- ¼ yd inner border
- ¾ yd outer border

BINDING
- ½ yd coordinating fabric

BACKING
- 1¼ yd coordinating fabric

ADDITIONAL TOOLS
- glue stick, freezer paper

SAMPLE QUILT
- **Red & Whites** by michael miller
- **Bella Solids Bleached White (98) & Betty's Red (123)** by moda fabrics

1 pair 'em up

Choose (4) 10" square prints for hearts: 2 dark & 2 light. Pair each with a background print of the opposite value: pair dark hearts with light backgrounds, light hearts with dark backgrounds.

Cut a 10" pair in half twice: (4) 5" same-print pairs. Keep together in a stack. Repeat for all 10" pairs.

2 make a heart

Make 1 heart from each 10" pair. Use (2) 5" pairs from a stack. Iron a crease diagonally across the 5" background square. This is the sew line.

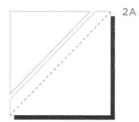

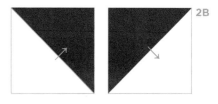

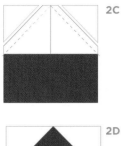

2C

2D

RST, sew on the fold. Trim ¼" away from the stitching: 1 HST. **2A** Repeat to make a second HST. Press 1 HST to the dark side; 1 HST to the light side. **2B**

From the remaining (2) 5" pairs, make the heart tops. Use:

  (2) 5" heart squares &
  (1) 5" background square

Cut the background square into (4) 2½" squares. Iron a diagonal sew line into each. Position (2) 2½" background squares on 2 adjacent corners of each 5" heart square. **2C** Sew across all squares on the diagonal as shown in the diagram. Trim off excess. Press out. **2D** Make 2.

3 construct heart

Arrange the (2) HSTs and (2) heart tops into a block. Repress (1) inside seam in row 1 to allow for better nesting and sharper points. Stitch the rows together first and press

according to the arrows. Then sew row 1 to row 2. Press. **3A** Repeat for a total of 4 heart blocks.

Block size: 9½" x 9½"

4 sashings & such

Cut (4) 1½" WOF strips from sashing fabric. Subcut (1) strip into (4) 9½" sashing segments.

Arrange the 4 heart blocks into a 2 x 2 setting. Sew the blocks together in rows with a 9½" sashing segment between them. **4A**

Cut a 1½" x 1½" cornerstone from the outer border fabric. Sew (2) 9½" sashing segments to either side of the cornerstone. Add this as horizontal sashing between the 2 rows of hearts. **4B**

5 borders

Use the remaining 1½" strips for the inner border. Follow steps in *construction basics* to attach to the quilt. **A-D** Press to the borders. **5A**

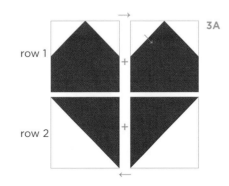

row 1

row 2

3A

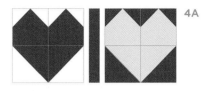

4A

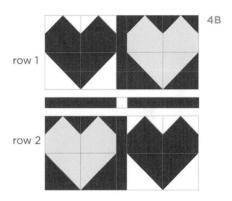

4B

row 1

row 2

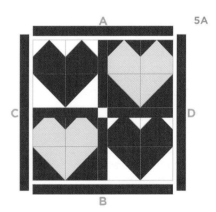

A   5A

C   D

B

A   5B

C   D

B

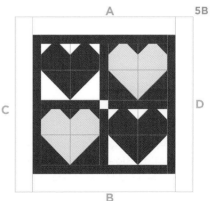

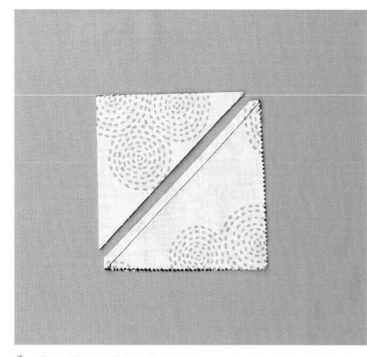

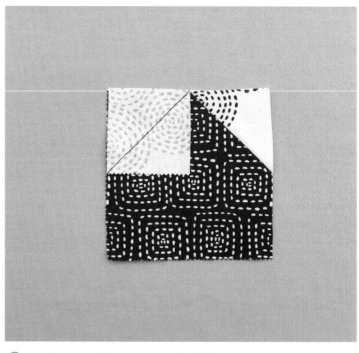

1   After pairing up a light & dark 10″ square and cutting it into (4) 5″ pairs, make (2) HSTs from 2 of the 4 pairs. Sew across the center diagonal and trim to ¼.″ Step 2.

2   For the tops of the hearts, use (2) 2½″ background squares on adjacent corners. Sew diagonally across each as shown; trim and press. Step 2.

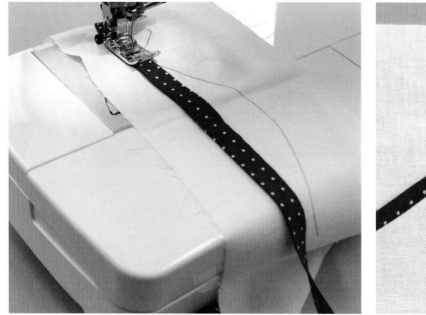

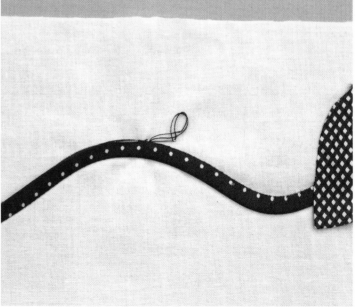

3   Trace or freehand draw a vine onto the border. Fold the 1½″ x 10″ bias rectangle in half lengthwise & press. With the raw edges following the vine, sew a ¼″ from the line. Move the bias strip into position as you sew. Step 6.

4   Take the folded edge of the bias strip and enclose the raw edges. Hand or machine stitch into place. Step 6.

Cut (4) 5″ WOF strips of outer border fabric. Attach to the quilt in the same manner as the inner border. **5B**

6 appliqué

Draw vines freehand or photocopy the vine diagram (shown at right) enlarging it by 200%. Cut along the solid line. Place the corner point 3¼″ from the inner border as measured on a 45° diagonal. **6A** Use a pencil or fabric marker to trace the shape onto the outer border, flipping the vine diagram to form the other side. Match the partial dotted line to first vine.

Cut (2) 1½″ x 10″ rectangles on the bias from each of (4) various 10″ squares. Fold them in half lengthwise and press.

Starting at the corner, lay the raw edges of the folded vine diagram along the traced vine as you sew a scant ¼″ from the traced line. Gently guide, do not pull the fabric.

Fold the strip over the raw edges and machine or hand stitch the folded edge to the outer border.

Trace a few large & small hearts onto freezer paper. **6B** Cut out and iron the shiny side to back of scrap fabric and/or various 10″ squares. Cut out around the shape. Reuse the freezer paper shapes to make a total of (20) large hearts & (16) small hearts.

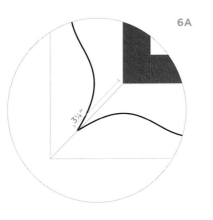

Use the glue stick to temporarily adhere the hearts to the vines. Make sure to cover all raw ends of the vines with a heart. Use a zig-zag, straight or blanket stitch to appliqué the hearts into place by machine.

7 quilt & bind

Layer quilt top on batting and backing and quilt the way you like. Square up all raw edges.

Cut (4) 2½″ strips from binding fabric to finish. See *construction basics* for greater detail.

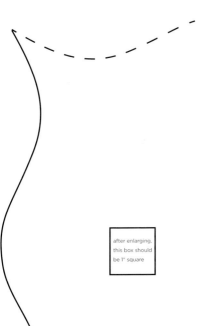

after enlarging, this box should be 1″ square

binding
tool *star*

designed by NOAH EARNHEART

I've made a quilt or two in my day, and I love to have tricks and shortcuts up my sleeve that help me work faster with better results. But I've got a learning curve just like everybody else, and you might laugh when I say that when we first opened the shop, I didn't know how to finish off a binding correctly. I read about it over and over and I just couldn't figure it out!

Sometimes it turns out the best trick to have is a real, live person from which to learn. I'm a very visual person and learn best from in-person interaction. So years ago when I went to quilt market and I saw a woman doing demonstrations of the perfect binding finish, I went up to her and asked, "Would you do that again? One more time? Can I film this?" Luckily that woman happened to be the fabulous Susan Brown and she just went along with it. We still have the tutorial on our YouTube channel.

For the tutorial and everything you need to make this quilt visit:
www.msqc.co/blockwinter15

Ever since that day when Susan was so patient and helpful to me, she has been a great friend to the Missouri Star Quilt Company. I was so excited to see her at the last quilt market, and when I saw that she had used her binding tool to make a star quilt, I loved the idea right away. Of course, I went right home and tried it myself, using her star for inspiration.

Next I turned to my teenage grandson, Noah, who came up with a whole quilt design for Susan's star. I get so

energized when I see what other quilters are doing, but even those who have never made a quilt can be amazing sources of inspiration too. I love this quilt because it reminds me that I can do great things when I rely on great friends. They say it takes a village to raise a child, and in my opinion it's the best way to make a quilt too!

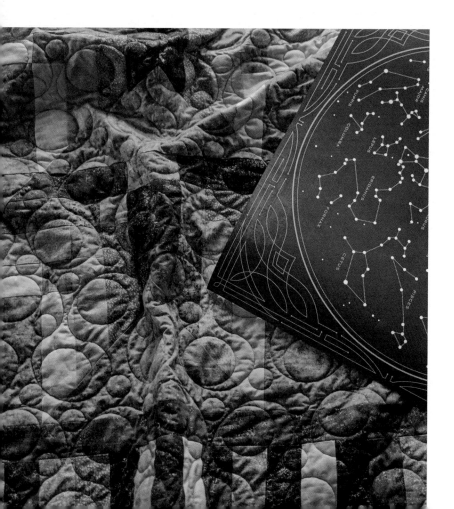

materials

makes a 78" X 78" quilt

QUILT TOP
- (1) 2½" WOF print roll
- (1) 5" square pack
- ½ yd inner border
- 2⅓ yds for background solid

BINDING
- ½ yd coordinating fabric

BACKING
- 3 yds coordinating fabric

ADDITIONAL TOOLS
- The Binding Tool by TQM rulers

SAMPLE QUILT
- **Artisan Spirit Blue Lagoon & Stonehenge Teal** by Stonehenge for Northcott Fabrics

1 cut

From the background fabric, cut:

(4) 8½" WOF strips; subcut into
    (16) 8½" squares

(4) 2½" WOF strips; subcut into
    (64) 2½" cornerstones

(4) 8⅞" WOF strips; subcut into
    (16) 8⅞" squares; cut in half
    on the diagonal

Select (4) strips of different values (dark, medium, medium-light & light). Keep the strips folded in half. From each WOF strip, cut out the *Binding Tool* shape twice (4 shapes). Plus, cut (2) 5" rectangles & set aside. **1A** Repeat 8 times.

Each shape cut out of the strip will produce a **pair**: (1) left-angled & (1) right-angled

1A

1B

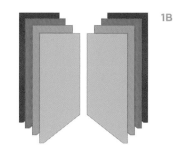

2A

2B

2C

2D

2 build the block

Using only the left-angled stack, add 2½″ cornerstones to the blunt ends of each shape. 2A Press to the cornerstone. Set these aside.

Begin with an 8½″ background square. Add a **light** right-angled shape to one side. 2B Press to the large square.

Select a same-print "2A" shape and add it to the adjacent side. 2C Nest the seams. Continue in this fashion with 4 prints—light to dark.

Attach (2) large background triangles to either side of the block. Make dog ears at the ¼″ seam allowance. Press to the outside. 2D Square up to 16½." Make 16 blocks.

Block Size: 16½″ x 16½″

shape. Set one pair from each strip aside for a second block. For each block, separate the pairs into (1) stack of left-angled shapes & (1) stack of right-angled shapes—4 per stack. 1B Make stacks for 16 blocks.

3A

3 construct rows

The quilt center consists of 4 rows of 4 blocks. Each row has 2 blocks pointing down to the right, and 2 blocks pointing down to the left. 3A

Work with 2 rows at a time. Sew blocks together side-to-side. Press the seams to the right on the top row; to the left on the bottom row. Sew the rows together. Nest seams. Make (2) 2-row units.

Flip (1) 2-row unit upside down and sew the row units together. Nest seams. Press horizontal seams to the quilt center.

Quilt Center Size: 64½″ x 64½″

4 inner border

From the inner border fabric cut (7) 2½″ strips. Follow steps in *construction basics* to attach to the quilt. A-D Press to the borders.

5 piano border

In addition to the (64) 2½″ x 5″ rectangles cut from WOF strips, cut all the 5″ squares in half once.
Total: (148) 2½″ x 5″ rectangles

Piece (34) 2½″ x 5″ rectangles together randomly lengthwise. Press all seams in the same direction. Make 2. Measure the quilt top width and cut the pieced borders to that size. Attach to the top & bottom of the quilt. Press to the inner border.

Repeat the same process, but use (39) rectangles for each side border. Measure and cut the borders to size. Attach and press to the inner border.

1 Select (1) 8½" square and (1) light-colored right-angled shape. Match the long side of the shape to the square a sew right sides together (RST). See 2B.

2 Attach a solid cornerstone to the blunt end of all left-angled shapes. Step 2.

3 Attach the second shape with its cornerstone to the adjacent side of the square and sew. Nest seams. Continue in this fashion until 4 cornerstones have been added to the block. Step 2.

4 Attach the (2) 8⅞" triangles to either side of the block. Square up to 16½." Step 2.

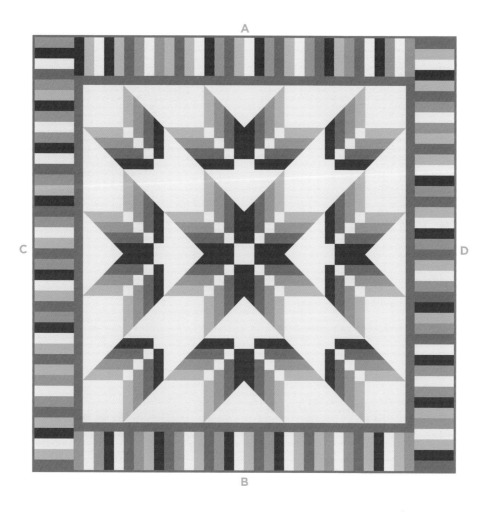

6 quilt & bind

Layer quilt top on batting and backing and quilt the way you like. Square up all raw edges.

Cut (8) 2½" strips from binding fabric to finish. See *construction basics* for greater detail.

flying geese
log cabin

quilt designed by JENNY DOAN

I love being out in the woods. The delicious scent of pine, the good, clean dirt, the night skies filled to bursting with starlight; it's all so peaceful and heavenly. Since my childhood traipsing along the edges of the mountains of California, the thought of living in a log cabin deep in the forest has been so appealing to me - the tranquility, the peaceful simplicity of it all. Well, that dream is yet to be realized, so for now, I have to be satisfied with the Log Cabin Quilt!

Countless quilts have passed through my hands over the years, but the Log Cabin Quilt is one of my very favorites. And the reason it is so special to me it that it is the first quilt I ever made!

Years ago, I took a quilting class at our local VoTech in Chillicothe, Missouri. The teacher was a cute young gal named Sherrie. I remember being surprised that a quilting instructor could be so young. I don't know why, but I just always thought that only old people quilted. Boy, was I wrong!

For the tutorial and everything you need to make this quilt visit:
www.msqc.co/blockwinter15

Sherrie taught with optimistic enthusiasm and her "can-do" attitude was contagious. She gave me confidence that I could succeed, so I jumped in with both feet and fell in love instantly.

Right away one of my favorite things about quilting was the creativity it afforded me. I started with the basic Log Cabin block and as I grew more comfortable, I wanted to see what would happen if I made little changes here and there. It was so fun to see how one simple alteration to the block could result in a totally different look!

> "Right away one of my favorite things about quilting was the creativity it afforded me."

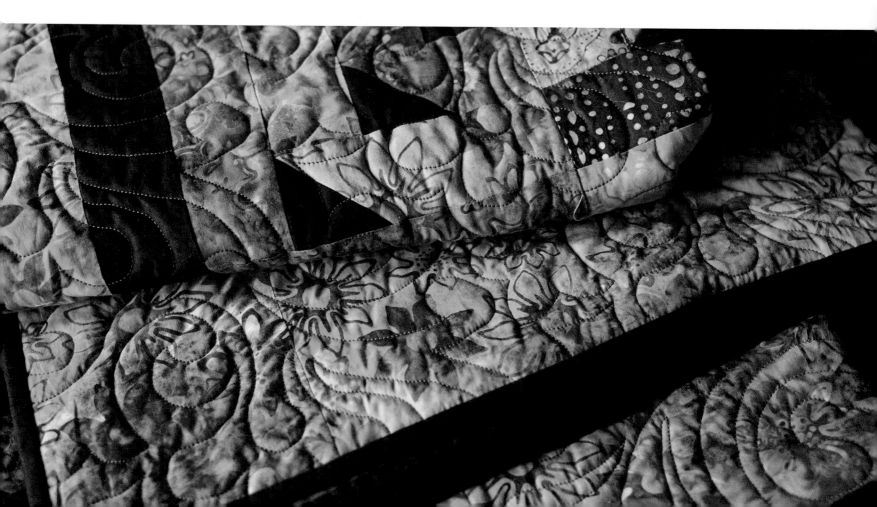

Years later I still love to experiment with the Log Cabin block. There are so many variations, each one as beautiful as the next. One day as I was playing around with the block, I decided to see what would happen if I snowballed one corner. I realized that if I repeated that snowballed corner with every two strips, I would end up with a really cool block. When I was finished, I stepped back to admire my work. That's when I noticed how much all those little triangles looked like flying geese. And thus, the Flying Geese Log Cabin Quilt was born.

I still don't live in the woods, but I wonder how many more variations of the Log Cabin Quilt I can come up with before I get my own real cabin (hint, hint, Honey)!

materials

makes a 64" X 80" quilt

QUILT TOP
- (1) 2½" print roll
- 1½ yds inner border/solid
- 1¼ yds outer border

BINDING
- ¾ yd coordinating fabric

BACKING
- 5 yds coordinating fabric

SAMPLE QUILT
- **Calypso** by Moda Fabrics
- **Bella Solids Black (99)** by Moda Fabrics

1 cut

From the solid fabric, cut:

    (12) 2½" WOF strips; subcut into

        (16) 2½" squares per strip

These are the "geese."

2 build the block

Iron a diagonal fold into (4) solid geese. This is the sewing line.

Cut a 2½" square from a print strip. RST, sew the solid & print squares together on the diagonal crease. **2A** Trim excess fabric ¼" from the stitching. Press to the solid. **2B**

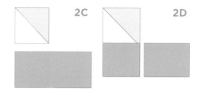

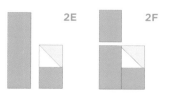

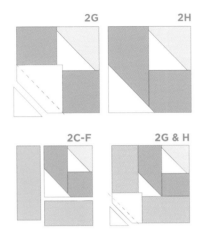

2G   2H

2C-F   2G & H

2I

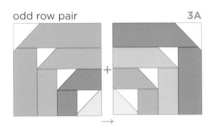

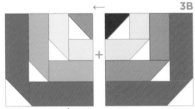

odd row pair   3A

even row pair   3B

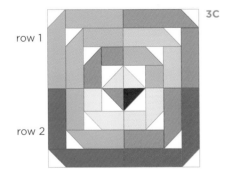

row 1

row 2

3C

Use a modified log cabin technique throughout. Build out the goose's corner by adding (2) print strips to either side. Then add another goose to the new corner. Always press to the strips & the geese.

2C: Select another 2½" print strip and attach to one side of the solid goose.

2D: Trim to the size of the block.

2E: Add the same print fabric strip to the adjacent side of the solid goose.

2F: Trim strip. Press to the strip.

2G: Sew a solid 2½" goose across the corner just created.

2H: Trim & press out.

Repeat **2C** through **2H** until there are 4 geese total in the block.

Block size: 8½" x 8½"   **2I**
Make 48 blocks.

3 arrange

Arrange the blocks in a 6 x 8 setting. Every pair of 2 blocks will have the geese pointing away from each other, i.e. 1 & 2, 3 & 4, etc. **3A**

In odd rows the pairs point up; in even rows they point down. **3A-B**

Every group of 4 blocks will form a multi-colored hourglass-on-point in the center. **3C**

4 construct center

Sew blocks together across side-to-side to form rows. Press seams in odd rows to one side; to the opposite side in even rows.

Sew rows together nesting seams as you go. Press horizontal seams to the center.

Quilt Center Size: 48½" x 64½"

5 borders

From the inner border fabric cut (6) 2½" strips. Follow steps in *construction basics* to attach to the quilt. **A-D** Press to the borders.

Cut (7) 6" strips of outer border fabric. Attach to the quilt in the same manner as the inner border.

6 quilt & bind

Layer quilt top on batting and backing and quilt the way you like. Square up all raw edges.

Cut (8) 2½" strips from binding fabric to finish. See *construction basics* for greater detail.

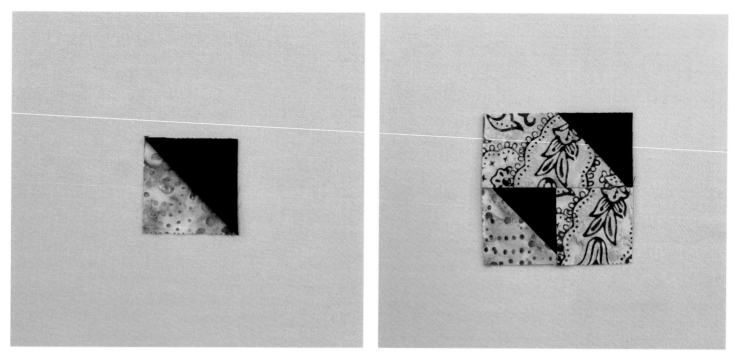

1   To begin a block, make a 2½″ HST from print and solid 2½″ squares. Step 2.

2   Select a second print and add strips to either side of the flying goose. Then add a second goose to that print's corner. Step 2.

3   Repeat with a third strip of another print adding the goose to the same corner. Step 2.

4   The block is complete with 4 different prints and 4 solid geese. Step 2.

A

C   D

B

55

Intersection
quilt

designed by NATALIE EARNHEART

I haven't always lived in a small town, but I like to think I've always been a small town kind of gal. We lived in a pretty big city in California when the kids were very small, but that didn't stop us from having a close relationship with our community. We jumped right in and participated in everything we could to make ourselves a part of that city.

One of our braver adventures was a frequent trip to the city library. You see, we didn't just pile in the car to get there. We biked. I had a three-wheeled bike with a basket in the back between the two rear wheels, and that's where the two smallest children rode along with me. All the rest of the clan kept up on their own bikes, even the little ones. We really must have been something to look at on those trips. Sometimes I think folks on the street thought we were a parade!

For the tutorial and everything you need to make this quilt visit:
www.msqc.co/blockwinter15

It didn't matter if it made us stand out or seem peculiar. That's the kind of thing I've always loved to do: round up the kids, pack a lunch, grab our quilts, and get out there where you can see the town, have adventures, and bump into your neighbors. That's one of many reasons why when we moved our gang to the Midwest, we absolutely fell in love with our little town. In many ways it's been this small-town gal's dream come true: parades, festivals, movies in the park, and best of all, knowing your neighbors by name! There's simply nothing like small town America.

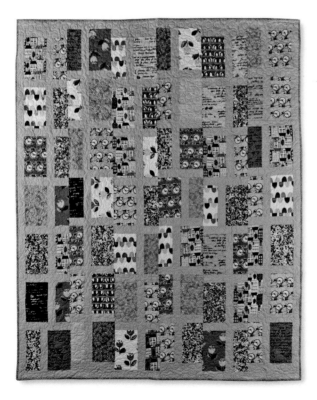

"Sometimes I think folks on the street thought we were a parade!"

materials
makes a 71" X 85½" quilt

QUILT TOP
- (1) 10" print pack
- (1) 2½" WOF roll solid

BINDING
- ¾ yd coordinating fabric

BACKING
- 5¼ yds coordinating fabric

SAMPLE QUILT
- **Our Town** by Michele D'Amour for Contempo

- **Kona Cottons Ash (1007)** by Robert Kaufman

1 cut

There are 42 blocks in the quilt.

From the 2½" WOF strips, subcut:
   (11) into 2½" x 10" segments &
   (14) into 2½" x 11½" segments

Use (42) 10" squares. Cut *each* into:
   (1) 6" x 10" rectangle &
   (1) 4" x 10" rectangle **1A**
Keep all the segments & rectangles sorted by size in separate stacks.

 TIP: *keep the blocks in the same orientation when adding the "T."*

 1A

 2A

 2B

 2C

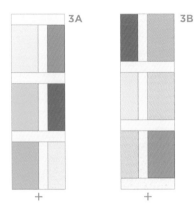

3A 3B

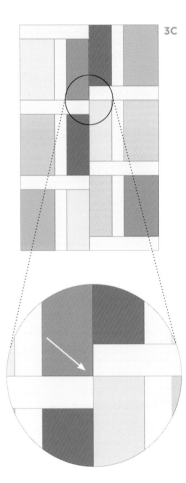

3C

2 build the block

Sew a 2½″ x 10″ solid segment to each of the 6″ x 10″ rectangles. **2A**

This a good time to *chain piece*. Chain piecing is a quick method of sewing blocks together. Feed a segment and rectangle RST through the sewing machine with a ¼″ seam. Continue sewing off the fabric a few stitches and feed the next pair of fabrics through the machine and so on. Snip threads to separate blocks.

Press to the solid strips throughout construction. Add a 4″ x 10″ rectangle in a different print to the other side of the solid strip. Chain piece all the blocks. **2B**

Next add a solid 2½″ x 11½″ segment to the top of the all the blocks forming a "T." **2C** Chain piece again.

It is important to keep the block orientation exactly the same.

Block size: 11½″ x 12″
Make 42 blocks.

3 arrange & sew

Arrange all the blocks into a 6 x 7 setting. Blocks in the odd-numbered columns have the "T" standing up **3A**; blocks in even-numbered columns have the "T" upside down. **3B**

Try for an overall even blend of light & dark fabrics. A design wall, open floor or large table will help in laying out the quilt top.

Sew blocks together top-to-bottom in columns. Again press seams to the solid segments.

Sew columns together nesting seams as you go. **3C** Press long vertical seams toward the quilt center.

Quilt Center Size: 66½″ x 81″

4 border

Use (8) 2½″ WOF solid strips for the final border. Follow steps in *construction basics* to attach to the quilt. **A-D** Press to the borders.

5 quilt & bind

Layer quilt top on batting and backing and quilt the way you like. Square up all raw edges.

Cut (9) 2½″ strips from binding fabric to finish. See *construction basics* for greater detail.

 TIP: *The quilt can also be sewn together in rows—just remember to press seams in alternate directions from row to row for better nesting.*

1 Cut all the 10" squares into (1) 6" and (1) 4" rectangle. Step 1.

2 Attach a solid 2½" x 10" segment to the long side of a 6" rectangle. Step 2.

3 Add a 4" rectangle of a different print to the solid strip. Step 2.

4 Keeping all blocks oriented the same (6" rectangle on the left) add the longer solid segment to the top of the block. Step 2.

5 The block now has a solid offset "T" and measures 11½" x 12." Step 2.

6 If you sew the quilt center together in rows, the "T" will switch from right side up to upside down from block to block. If you sew the quilt center together in columns, all blocks right side up are in odd columns; upside down in even columns. Step 3.

A

C

D

B

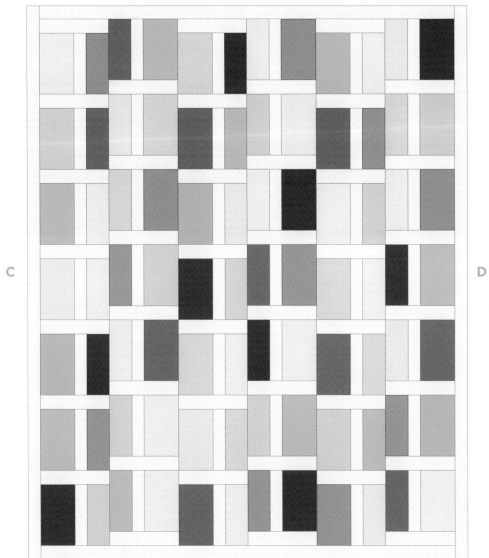

For the tutorial and everything you need to make this quilt visit:
www.msqc.co/blockwinter15

paper *stories*

quilt designed by JENNY DOAN

Whenever I see horse fabric, I am reminded of the infamous "Worst Doan Family Bedtime Story of All Time."

It's wasn't my fault, really. As the mother of seven young children, my steam usually ran out right around five o'clock in the evening. Up until then I did a pretty good job of wrangling the mob, working through the noise, and generally managing the chaos created by my seven little people. We played, we worked, we sang, we read. It really was a wonderful life! Exhausting, but wonderful.

But as afternoon turned to evening, our crazy little heaven usually started to fall apart. By then the kids were tired, hungry, and anxious for Dad to get home from work, so things would get a little wild. By the time the clock struck five, my patience and energy would have reached their limits and I'd feel completely spent. On a good day, I would already have dinner in the slow cooker or a casserole all made up and ready to pop in the oven.

"Once upon a time there was a beautiful horse. And he loved to run. . . and one day he stepped in a hole and broke his leg. And so they shot him. 'Night kids!"

But there were many days that we'd end up with a quick and easy meal of cereal or sandwiches. Evening just wasn't my best time.

One night my husband thought it would be a good idea for me to tell the kids a bedtime story. I told him firmly that I was way too tired for stories. But he looked at me with those puppy dog eyes and batted his lashes (Why do men always have the best lashes?), so I said I would try.

I sat down on the bed, closed my weary eyes, and began,

"Once upon a time there was a beautiful horse. And he loved to run. And he would run around and around with his mane flying behind him. And one day he stepped in a hole and broke his leg. And so they shot him. 'Night kids!!"

My children just sat there in stunned silence as I bolted out of the room giggling like a sleep-starved maniac. I came a few minutes later with a "juuust kidding"...what actually happened is, "The sweet horse went to a wonderful horse hospital, got all fixed up, and lived out the rest of his days in a beautiful field of wildflowers, where a family of happy children brushed him and fed him apples every day."

The children recovered and went to sleep with smiles on their faces and my husband never asked me to do bedtime stories ever again.

Even though this was years and years ago, the kids have never forgotten this story or let me forget it. In my defense, though, it was late and I was tired! I can't be held responsible!

materials

makes a 62½" X 72" quilt

QUILT TOP
- (1) 2½" WOF print roll
- 1½ yds inner border/accent solid
- 1¼ yds outer border

BINDING
- ¾ yd coordinating fabric

BACKING
- 4 yds coordinating fabric

ADD'L MATERIALS
- MSQC 10" Paper Piecing Squares
- lapel glue stick

SAMPLE QUILT
- **Derby Style** by Melissa Mortenson for Riley Blake
- **Bella Solids Gray (83)** by Moda Fabrics

1 cut

From the inner border/accent solid fabric, cut:

(21) 2½" WOF strips;
set aside (6) for Step 5.

2 build the block

Use a *MSQC 10" Paper Piecing* square and the lapel glue stick. The goal is to cover the 10" square with 2½" diagonal strips, then use the paper as a pattern to square up the block.

Lay down a diagonal stripe of glue onto a 10" paper. The paper will be hard to remove later if too much glue is applied. **2A**

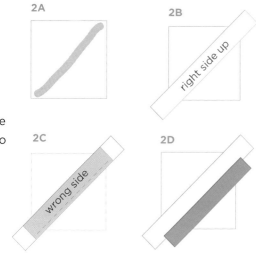

2A

2B
right side up

2C
wrong side

2D

2E

3A

3B

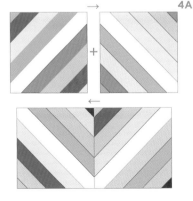

4A

Place a solid strip *right side up* onto the glue. This will hold the strip in place as you work. Make sure the strip covers the paper. 2B

Select a 2½" WOF print strip. Right sides together (RST), sew it to the first strip along its length—no need to sew beyond the paper however. 2C Press open. 2D

Continue adding print strips to both sides of the center solid strip until the paper is covered entirely (approx. 6-8 print strips). 2E

TIP cut (60) 14" sections from the print roll at the start. This way you won't run out of longer sections.

3 trim
Flip the block to the back and trim all the strips to the paper edge. 3A Reuse the scraps for other blocks. Remove the paper at this point.

Block size: 10" x 10" 3B
Make 30 blocks.

4 arrange & sew
Lay the blocks into a 5 x 6 setting. Turn the blocks so that the center solid strips form a diamond shape when 4 blocks come together. The solid strips

are not meant to match perfectly. 4A

Sew blocks together side-to-side across to build a row. Press seams in odd rows to one side; in even rows to the opposite side. Sew rows together nesting seams. Press horizontal seams in one direction.

Quilt Center Size: 48" x 57½"

5 borders
For the inner border use the solid 2½" strips that were set aside. Follow steps in *construction basics* to attach to the quilt. A-D Press to the borders.

Cut (7) 5½" strips of outer border fabric. Attach to the quilt in the same manner as the inner border.

6 quilt & bind
Layer quilt top on batting and backing and quilt the way you like. Square up all raw edges.

Cut (8) 2½" strips from binding fabric to finish. See *construction basics* for greater detail.

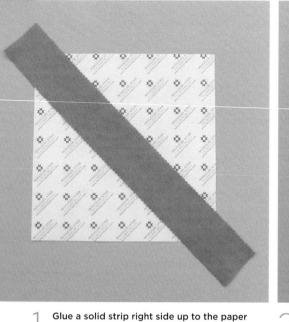

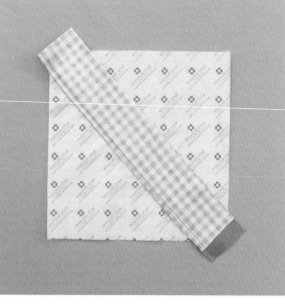

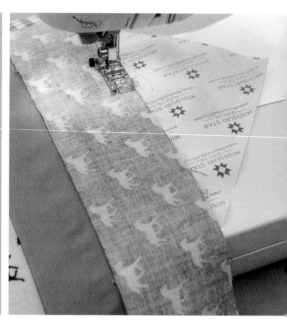

1 Glue a solid strip right side up to the paper square on the diagonal. Step 2.

2 Right sides together (RST) add a print strip to one side and sew them together right through the paper. Step 2.

3 Continue adding print strips until the entire 10" paper square is covered in fabric. Step 2.

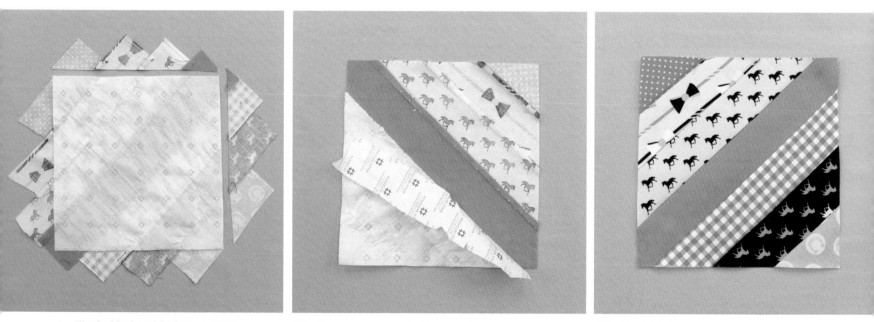

4 Flip the block upside down and trim away the excess fabric using the paper square as a pattern. Step 3.

5 Remove the paper. It will tear easily along the lines of stitching. Step 3.

6 The finished block will measure 10" x 10" and have 6-8 print strips total. Save any leftover strips for other blocks. Step 3.

A

C

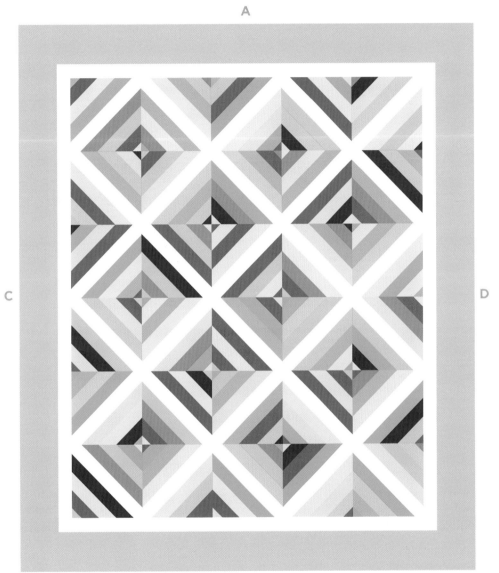

D

B

For the tutorial and everything
you need to make this quilt visit:
www.msqc.co/blockwinter15

tipsy
tumbler

designed by NATALIE EARNHEART

When our kids were growing up, Ron and I did our best to say "yes" when they asked to do something as a family. Sometimes that meant getting creative and working around circumstances. One year, for example, I remember the kids were hounding us to go camping. We love camping, but it was still early spring and too cold to go on an outside adventure. So we did what any rational parents would do: we set up camp in the living room! One tent for the boys, one for the girls, and one for Ron and me, all facing toward each other.

There was no fishing on that camping trip, no hiking, and a lot less dirt than usual. (Notice I didn't say there wasn't any dirt. With kids it seems like there's always dirt from somewhere.) But even without all the trappings of a traditional camping trip, we made a good time for ourselves. We swapped stories around the "fire" (a flashlight pointing at the ceiling), snacked on trail mix, and above all else, we sang.

Singing is our family's favorite camping tradition, and even if the quality of the singing can be wanting, we do it with gusto. And combining singing with our love of games takes everything to the next level.

Our family has a game where we pick a word and each team has to come up with a song that has that word in it, going back and forth until we can't think of any more. As you might imagine, as the teams segregated into girls versus boys, the competition was fierce. It was easy enough with words like "love" and "girl" but the kids usually came up with far more ridiculous words than that, and I'm sure you can imagine how tricky things got from there. (You'd never believe how many songs have the word 'cow' in them.)

The beauty of a family camp-in is that you don't need any special equipment. No tents or sleeping bags required. Just grab a quilt and get creative. Some of my best memories happened in a blanket fort!

" The beauty of a family camp-in is that you don't need any special equipment. No tents or sleeping bags required. Just grab a quilt and get creative. "

materials

makes a 56" X 63½" quilt

QUILT TOP
• (1) 5" square pack print
• (1) 10" square pack solid
• 1 yd border fabric

BINDING
• ½ yd coordinating fabric

BACKING
• 3½ yds coordinating fabric

ADD'L TOOLS
• MSQC 5" Tumbler Shape

SAMPLE QUILT
• **Camp Cozy** by Quilting Treasures
• **Bella Solids White (98)** by Moda Fabrics

1 cut & select

With the *MSQC 5" Tumbler Tool* cut a tumbler shape from each of the (42) 5" print squares. 1A

1A

2A

2B

2 tip the tumbler

Set a print tumbler on a 10" background solid square at any angle. **2A** Fold the background fabric over the tumbler along one side. **2B** Press. Sew a ¼" seam on the fold. Press open. **2C** Repeat for the opposite side. **2D-E**

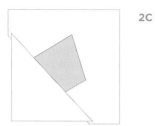

2C

2D

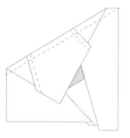

2E

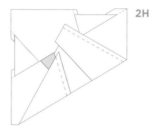

2F

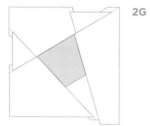

2G

2H

2I

2J

Repeat folding and sewing for the top & bottom. **2F-I** Square up to 8." **2J**

Block size: 8" x 8"

3 arrange & sew

Arrange the blocks in an eye-pleasing 6 x 7 setting.

Build rows first by sewing blocks together side-to-side across. Press seams in all odd rows in one direction; in all even rows in the opposite direction.

Sew rows together nesting seams as you go to complete the quilt center. Press horizontal seams to the center.

Quilt Center size: 45½" x 53"

4 border

From the outer border fabric cut (6) 5½" strips. Follow steps in *construction basics* to attach to the quilt. **A-D** Press to the borders.

5 quilt & bind

Layer quilt top on batting and backing and quilt the way you like. Square up all raw edges.

Cut (7) 2½" strips from binding fabric to finish. See *construction basics* for greater detail.

1 Cut tumbler shapes from 5″ print squares. Step 1.

2 Set the tumbler on a 10″ background solid square at any angle.

3 Work with opposite sides. Fold the background fabric over the tumbler matching the tumbler fabric's angled side. Sew a ¼″ seam along the fold. Repeat with the opposite side. Step 2.

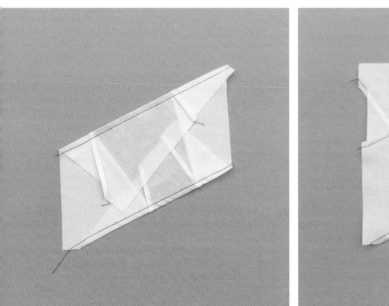

4 Repeat the same process with the top and bottom sides of the tumbler. Step 2.

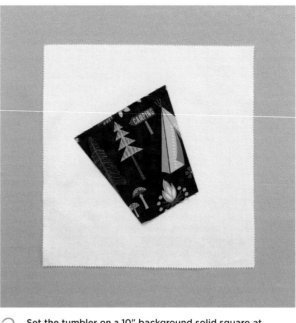

5 The tumbler is now sewn completely to the background square. Step 2.

6 Trim the block to 8″ square. Step 2.

A

C   D

B

spring
dresdens

designed by JENNY DOAN

Every spring I watch the temperature like a hawk.
As soon as the threat of frost has passed, I start
planting flowers on my porch. We have a wonderful
wrap-around porch and I love to fill it to bursting
with flowers. I have always adored beautiful plants.
They just make me happy.

In the early years of our marriage, my sweet
husband loved to surprise me with flowers. Ever the
romantic, Ron would spend way too much money
on stunning bouquets of expensive roses, lilies,
and hydrangeas. And each and every time, I would
thank him, give him a kiss, and then say with a smile,
"Next time, get me something with roots."

For the tutorial and everything you need to make this quilt visit:
www.msqc.co/blockwinter15

Finally, one day, Ron presented me with a flat of pansies. I was ecstatic! Ron watched me in disbelief as I excitedly grabbed my gloves and shovel and proceeded to plant them all over the yard.

"Really? These pansies make you happy?" he asked.

"YES!"

"You know, it only cost me six bucks for the whole flat. Do they still make you happy?"

"Of course! They are gorgeous, and best of all, they will last all summer long!"

Well, I think Ron learned a lesson that day. Now, every year when spring arrives, you can find the two of us down at the local nursery picking up flat after flat of flowers to plant. I do still enjoy the occasional fancy bouquet, but I'll always prefer flowers that stick around long enough to really be enjoyed. Of course the longest lasting flowers of all are these adorable quilted Dresden flowers. No other flower has such lasting beauty that it can be passed down and admired for generations!

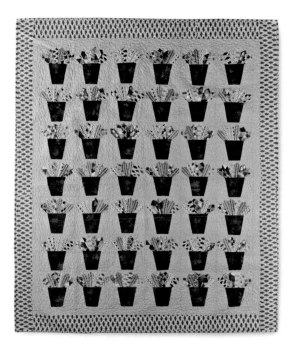

"I do still enjoy the occasional fancy bouquet, but I'll always prefer flowers that stick around long enough to really be enjoyed."

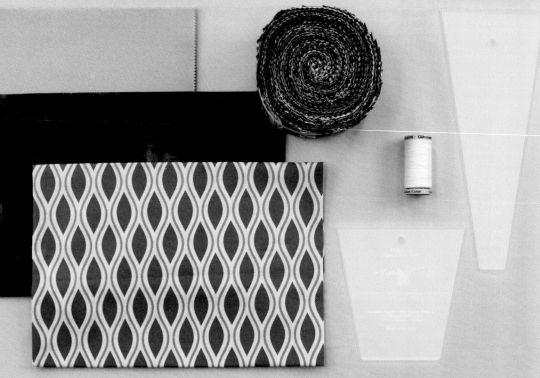

materials

makes a 71" X 80½" quilt

QUILT TOP
- (1) 10" square pack solid
- (3) 5" square packs prints
- 1¼ yd for flower pots

BINDING
- ½ yd coordinating fabric

BACKING
- 5 yds coordinating fabric

ADD'L TOOLS
- MSQC Dresden Plate Tool
- MSQC 5" Tumbler Tool
- Heat 'n Bond fusible **OR** lapel stick

SAMPLE QUILT
- **Kinetic** by Another Point of View for Windham Fabrics
- **Grunge Plum (243)** by Moda Fabrics
- **Bella Solids Gray (83)** by Moda Fabrics

1 cut

If you choose to use *Heat 'n Bond*, press it to the wrong side of the flower pot fabric following the product instructions.

Cut (5) 5" WOF strips from the flower pot fabric. Use the *MSQC 5" Tumbler Tool* to cut shapes from the strips. Make sure to flip the shape as you cut the strips. It's quicker and saves fabric too! **1A** Make 42 background tumblers.

With the *MSQC Dresden Plate Tool* cut (2) dresden shapes from each 5" square. **1B** Use the narrow end.

1A

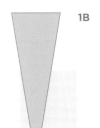

1B

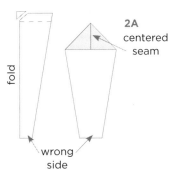

2A
centered
seam

fold

wrong
side

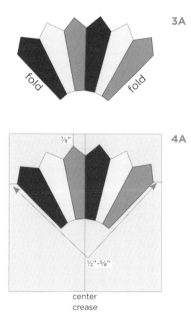

3A

4A

⁷⁄₈″

½″-⅝″

center
crease

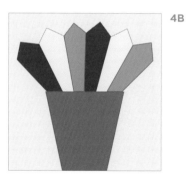

4B

2 sew the petals

Shorten the machine's stitch length to 1.5-2.0 stitches per inch. Fold "petal" in half lengthwise RST. Sew across the top at the widest end. Chain piece all the petals. Clip the seam allowance 45° at the folded edge to reduce bulk. Turn the corner right side out, pushing the seam allowance to one side. Flip to the back. Center the seam down the middle

creating a point. **2A** Press. Repeat for all flower "petals."

3 make flowers

Randomly sew 6 petals together side-by-side using a ¼″ seam. Press seams to the same side, strengthening the seam. Turn under the raw edges of each side ¼″ and press. **3A** Make 42.

4 pot the flowers

For a centering line, fold a 10″ background square in half once and press. Line up the seam between petals 3 & 4 of the dresden flower to the folded line. Check the position with a tumbler "pot" lined up on the bottom edge. Ours was ⁷⁄₈″ from the top, and ½″-⅝″ from each side. Pin or glue the flowers into place. **4A**

Appliqué the flower into place along its sides and zig-zag points. Use a neutral thread color & sew either by hand or machine. A blanket, straight or zig-zag stitch is recommended for machine appliqué.

Reposition the pot so it sits on the bottom of the square and covers the raw-edge ends of the flowers. Fuse or glue into place. Appliqué around the sides and top of the pot in the same manner as the flowers. **4B**

Block size: 10″ x 10″

5 arrange & sew

Lay out the blocks in an eye-pleasing 6 x 7 setting.

Build rows first by sewing blocks together side-to-side across. Press seams in all odd rows in one direction; in all even rows in the opposite direction.

Sew rows together nesting seams as you go to complete the quilt center. Press horizontal seams to the center.

Quilt Center Size: 57½″ x 67″

6 borders

From the inner border fabric cut (7) 2½″ strips. Follow steps in *construction basics* to attach to the quilt. **A-D** Press to the borders.

Cut (8) 5″ strips of outer border fabric. Attach to the quilt in the same manner as the inner border.

7 quilt & bind

Layer quilt top on batting and backing and quilt the way you like. Square up all raw edges.

Cut (8) 2½″ strips from binding fabric to finish. See *construction basics* for greater detail.

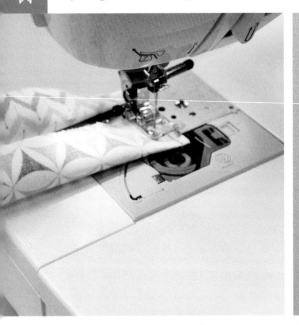

1 Reduce your machine's stitch length to 1.5-2.0. Chain piece the folded "petals" across their widest end. Step 2.

2 Randomly select petals and sew them side-to-side with a ¼" seam. Step 3.

3 Press. Sew 3 pairs together to make a flower. Step 3.

4 Press all seams of a flower in the same direction. Fold the sides under a ¼" and press. Step 3.

5 Center the flowers on a 10" solid square. You can finger press a fold in the square as a guideline to help with positioning. Check the position with a flower pot. Pin or glue in place. Appliqué around the top and sides by hand or machine. Step 4.

6 Fuse or glue the pot onto the square making sure to capture the raw ends of the petals. Step 4. Appliqué the pot in the same manner as the flowers.

A

C 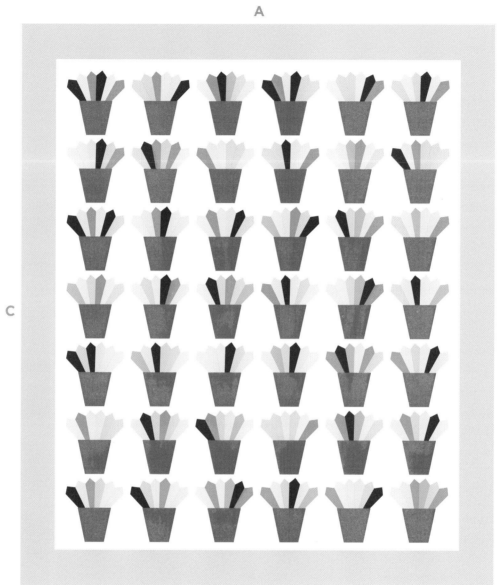 D

B

How to appliqué

To appliqué is to put on or apply a shape or cut out to a larger piece of fabric. Some of the ladies in our sewing group refer to it as the "A" word! We are here to calm your nerves and give you options! Aside from being fun and innovative, appliqué takes your quilt designs to a whole new level! Most appliqué will fall into the following two categories: hand or needle-turn appliqué and machine appliqué.

Hand appliqué, as the name suggests, means that you stitch the fabric down using your needle and thread. Machine appliqué, on the other hand, involves using your sewing machine to attach the fabric shape to your quilt. There are countless methods for getting a piece of fabric to behave and stay in place using whichever method of appliqué you choose. We'll share a few of our favorites.

Freezer Paper

Everyday freezer paper is great for appliqué. The waxy shiny side will adhere temporarily to material, making it possible to transfer shapes accurately and easily. Just be careful not to touch the shiny side of the paper with your iron, or you'll have a waxy mess on your iron surface!

First, trace your pattern or shape onto the freezer paper. (Be sure to reverse the image if needed when making letters or numbers). Cut

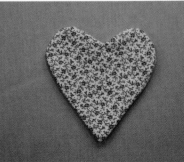

this shape out carefully using a sharp pair of scissors. This freezer paper shape can be reused several more times. Place the freezer paper templates shiny side to the wrong side of the fabric and cut about ¼ inch around the edge. Then, press the fabric around the edges of the template using spray starch and an iron to create a perfect shape. Remove the freezer paper, and you're ready to hand or machine stitch the appliqué piece to the background fabric.

Fusible Interfacing

The word fusible means "able to be fused or melted". It is a thin layer of glue that is activated by heat. Fusible Interfacing has a fusible layer on one side. You can tell which side is fusible by the look and feel - the fusible side will have a rough or bumpy texture. Having this type of material can make appliqué a breeze. To appliqué with fusible interfacing, cut out the shape from both the fabric and fusible interfacing, adding a 1/4-inch seam allowance. Place the right side of the fabric and the fusible side of the interfacing together. Sew around the shape, using a 1/4-inch seam allowance. Clip curves and trim corners as necessary to reduce bulk on the finished design. Cut a slit in the back of the interfacing and flip the appliqué right side out. Finger press the edges of your appliqué shape. (Don't iron the appliqué yet or you'll activate the fusible material and have a patch stuck to your ironing board!) If needed, use a point turner or stiletto to carefully push out corners or small areas that

aren't quite flat. Position the appliqué in place with the interfacing side down on your background. Lightly press, holding the iron in each spot only 3-4 seconds. Finally, stitch the appliqué in place by hand or machine.

Fusible Web

Heat 'n Bond is one of many fusible items on the market. It is a web-like product that has a paper backing. There are several similar products on the market carrying such names as "wonder under" or "fusible webbing," and the choice is yours which to buy. What's important to note is what a fusible web product actually is: a double-sided adhesive that glues two layers of fabric together.

To get a nice clean edge, its best to cut a piece of Heat 'n Bond that is slightly larger than your appliqué piece. Once you get that piece cut out, place the adhesive side down on the wrong side of the fabric and iron it down, placing the hot iron on the paper side of the adhesive. Hold it for a few minutes to be sure that the adhesive is activated, then cut your shape out of both the fabric and the paper. Remove the paper by scoring the back with a pin or scissor edge. Once you have a good starting point, the paper should peel right off. Place your appliqué piece directly on the fabric and double check it's in the right place before you set it with an iron. Press firmly in place and stitch down using a zig zag or blanket stitch.

Appliqué Glue

As odd as it may sound, glue can truly be a quilter's best friend! A touch of glue makes appliqué nice and easy. When appliqués are glued to the background fabric, there is very little shifting during the sewing process. There are many different types of appliqué glue on the market, but we love to use Lapel Stick to keep fabric in place for paper piecing and appliqué.

The method for using appliqué glue is similar to those of the previous methods in this article. Just cut your shape, be sure to reverse it if needed, and add a quarter of an inch of fabric all the way around. Dab a small bit of glue along the edge and fold the fabric a quarter of an inch to cover the glue. This will create a nice finished edge that will stay in place until your project is completed. Now, place your fabric on your quilt or project and add a dab of glue to hold it in place. Finish off your appliqué with a hand appliqué stitch or by machine.

As you see, appliqué is an incredibly useful technique that will elevate your quilts to the next level. Remember our challenge for the month: don't be afraid to try something new!

binding tool star

QUILT SIZE
78" X 78"

DESIGNED BY
Noah Earnheart

PIECED BY
Cindy Morris

QUILTED BY
Mary Bontrager

QUILT TOP
(1) 2½" WOF print roll
(1) 5" square pack
½ yd inner border
2⅓ yds for background solid

BINDING
½ yd coordinating fabric

BACKING
3 yds coordinating fabric

ADDITIONAL TOOLS
The Binding Tool by TQM rulers

SAMPLE QUILT
**Artisan Spirit Blue Lagoon &
Stonehenge Teal**
by Stonehenge for Northcott
Fabrics

ONLINE TUTORIALS
msqc.co/blockwinter15

QUILTING
Variety

QUILT PATTERN
pg 40

 TIP: *Want to make a different size? No problem, check out these and other patterns online!*

disappearing hourglass 2

QUILT SIZE
59" X 70¼"

DESIGNED BY
Jenny Doan

PIECED BY
Jenny Doan

QUILTED BY
Emma Jensen

QUILT TOP
1½ yds dark solid
1½ yds background solid
½ yd inner border
1 yd outer border

BINDING
½ yd coordinating fabric

BACKING
4 yds coordinating fabric

SAMPLE QUILT
Bella Solids White (98) & Sky (177)
by Moda Fabrics

ONLINE TUTORIALS
msqc.co/blockwinter15

QUILTING
Feather Meander

PATTERN
pg 16

flying geese log cabin

QUILT SIZE
64" X 80"

DESIGNED BY
Jenny Doan

PIECED BY
Kelly McKenzie

QUILTED BY
Sandi Gaunce

QUILT TOP
(1) 2½" print roll
1½ yds inner border/solid
1¼ yds outer border

BINDING
¾ yd coordinating fabric

BACKING
5 yds coordinating fabric

SAMPLE QUILT
Calypso by Moda Fabrics

Bella Solids Black (99)
by Moda Fabrics

ONLINE TUTORIAL
msqc.co/blockwinter15

QUILTING
Variety

PATTERN
pg 48

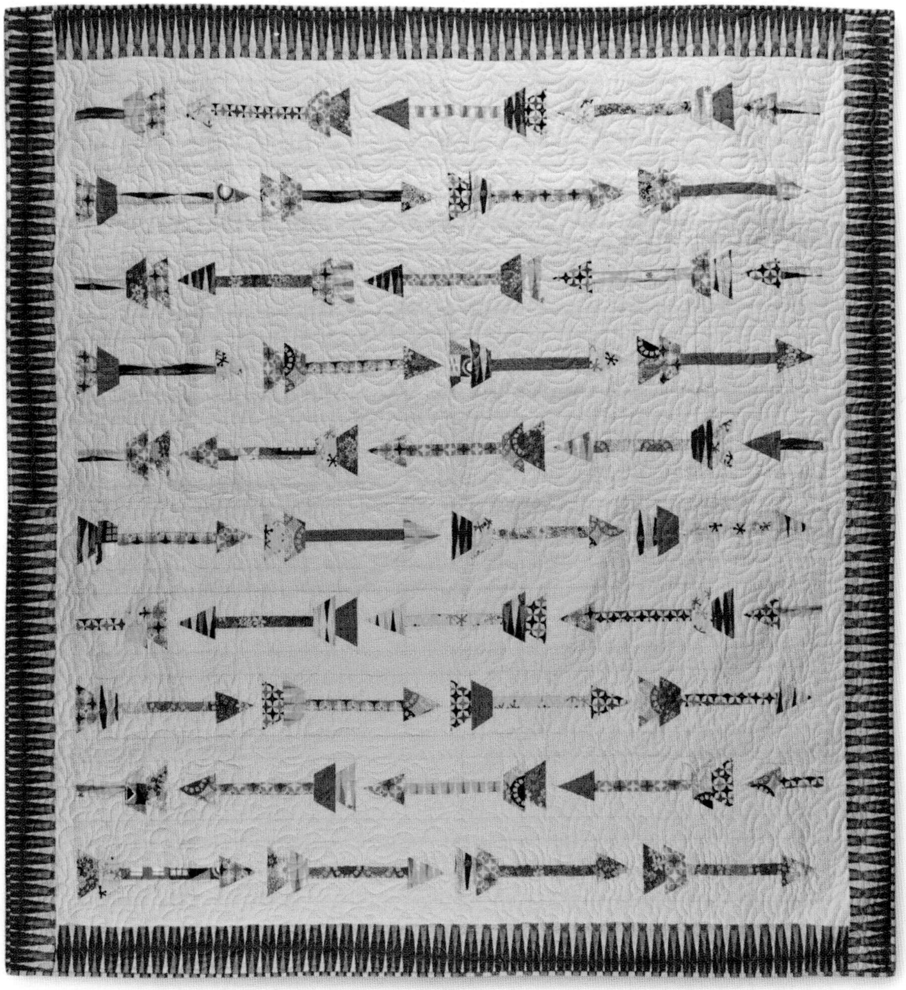

hit the mark

QUILT SIZE
86" X 87"

DESIGNED BY
Natalie Earnheart

PIECED BY
Cindy Morris

QUILTED BY
Jamey Stone

QUILT TOP
(1) 10" square pack print
2 yds background solid
1½ yds outer border

BINDING
¾ yd coordinating fabric

BACKING
8 yds 44" **OR** 2¾ yds 108"

ADDITIONAL TOOLS
MSQC 5" Half-Hexagon Shape
MSQC Small Simple Wedge

SAMPLE QUILT
Playful by Melody Miller of
Cotton + Steel for RJR

Bella Solids Natural (12) by
Moda Fabrics

ONLINE TUTORIALS
msqc.co/blockwinter15

QUILTING
Birds

QUILT PATTERN
pg 8

honey
do

QUILT SIZE
50½" X 63½"

DESIGNED BY
Natalie Earnheart

PIECED BY
Cindy Morris

QUILTED BY
Betty Bates

QUILT TOP
(1) 10" print pack
1 yd dark solid fabric

BINDING
¾ yd coordinating fabric

BACKING
3¼ yds coordinating fabric

ADDITIONAL TOOLS
10" MSQC Half Hexagon
Shape Tool

SAMPLE QUILT
Mixologie by Studio M for Moda
Fabrics
Bella Solids Navy (20) by Moda
Fabrics

ONLINE TUTORIALS
msqc.co/blockwinter15

QUILTING
Cottonseed

QUILT PATTERN
PG 24

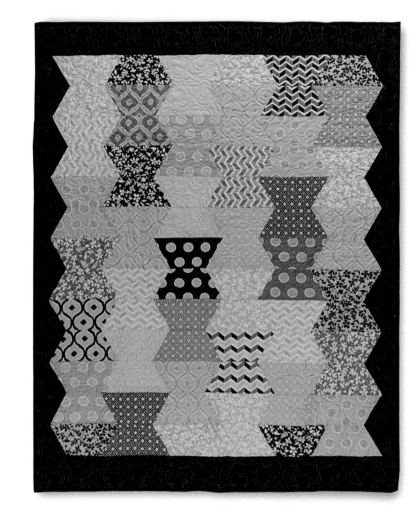

intersection

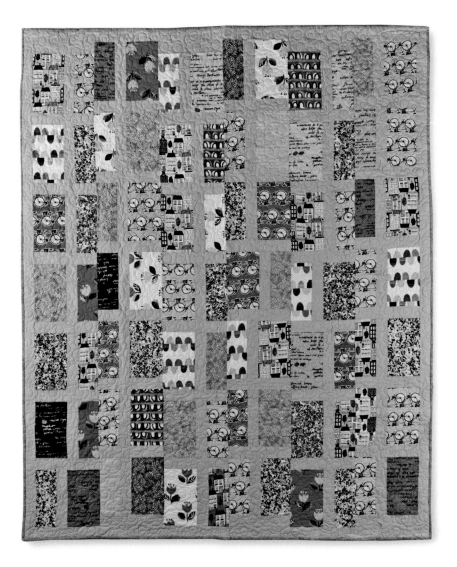

QUILT SIZE
71" X 85½"

DESIGNED BY
Natalie Earnheart

PIECED BY
Kelly McKenzie

QUILTED BY
Karen Russell

QUILT TOP
(1) 10" print pack
(1) 2½" WOF roll solid

BINDING
¾ yd coordinating fabric

BACKING
5¼ yds coordinating fabric

SAMPLE QUILT
Our Town by Michele
D'Amour for Contempo
Kona Cottons Ash (1007) by
Robert Kaufman

ONLINE TUTORIALS
msqc.co/blockwinter15

QUILTING
Loops & Swirls

PATTERN
PG 56

love is in the air

TABLE TOPPER/WALLHANGING SIZE
31" X 31"

DESIGNED BY
Jenny Doan

PIECED BY
Kelly McKenzie

QUILTED BY
Amy Gertz

QUILT TOP
(1) 10" pack of valentine-
themed prints
¼ yd inner border
¾ yd outer border

BINDING
½ yd coordinating fabric

BACKING
1¼ yd coordinating fabric

ADDITIONAL TOOLS
glue stick, freezer paper

SAMPLE QUILT
Red & Whites by michael miller
**Bella Solids Bleached White
(98) & Betty's Red (123)** by
moda fabrics

ONLINE TUTORIALS
msqc.co/blockwinter15

QUILTING
Hearts Large

QUILT PATTERN
PG 32